SWEETGRASS
II

Good fortune always!

Wayne Keon Oct/90

WORKS BY WAYNE KEON

Sweetgrass (poems, 1972)
with Ronald and Orville Keon
Thunderbirds of the Ottawa (a novel, 1977)
with Orville Keon

Sweetgrass II

POEMS

Wayne Keon

The Mercury Press
(an imprint of Aya Press)
Stratford, Ontario

The publisher gratefully acknowledges the financial assistance of the Canada Council and the Ontario Arts Council.

ACKNOWLEDGEMENTS:

Poems in *Sweetgrass II* have appeared or are forthcoming in:

Acta Victoriana, Ariel, Beneath the Surface, Breakthrough, Canadian Forum, Canadian Literature, Carousel, Cosmic Trend, Crone Papers, Dandelion, Exile, Fiddlehead, Grain, Green's Magazine, The Journal, Lines Review, Mainline, Malahat Review, Metropolitan Toronto Business Journal, The Moosehead Anthology, The New Quarterly, NeWest Review, Prism International, Sacred Climaxes (anthology), The Stump, Tabula Rasa, Toronto South Asian Review, UC Review, Waves, Whetstone.

Cover art: Ferguson Plain
Inside drawings: Wayne Keon
Production co-ordination: The Blue Pencil
Editor for the press: Beverley Daurio

Typeset in Berkeley Old Style and Gill Sans and printed and bound in Canada

Canadian Cataloguing in Publication:

Keon, Wayne
  Sweetgrass II : poems

ISBN 0-920544-78-9

I. Title.

PS8571.E65S84 1990   C811'.54   C90-095005-6
PR9199.3.K46S84 1990

Sales Representation: The Literary Press Group.

The Mercury Press is distributed in Canada by University of Toronto Press, and in the United States by Inland Book Company (selected titles) and Bookslinger.

The Mercury Press (an imprint of Aya Press)
Box 446
Stratford, Ontario
Canada N5A 6T3

To Bertholde Carter,
without whose healing and silver power,
these writings probably would not have emerged.

Contents

xiv

this nite
of all nites
in shining steel

drink,food
sweat,blood
cries nd feathers

of all things
leather bound
living once

my head becomes
a kind of a
rotary apparatus

reeling drunkenly
grinding images
thru a quik
motion shutter
set at 1/50000 sec

stopping
arresting
the mounted horseman
in mid gallop
demanding
to know what
is the image
what is the
object
what is the image
nd where is the
truth of the scene

in this village

in this village
this great
village

        i
        am no
        man's sun prophet

called canada
from the
tongue

        i can hardly
        manage my own
        day to day incidents

of my mother
earth ojibway
algonkin

        or resolve
        what's been past
        nd mystery of the sun

people of
long
ago

        i am standing
        before you
        sun

dream awakening

in
my dreams
the spirit horsemen

fly
upon the
sun bright on blue

sky
nd heavens
while all the people

are
watching
madly cheer

the race
will
end

no
winner
declared

all
because
the man raven

has
not yet
returned from

outside
my door the
cat is scratching

clawing
the wall
for something

to eat
for hunger
has awakened her

my
woman
has arisen

opens the door
nd plugs in the
elektrik kettle for koffee

travelin lite

travelin lite
by day
nd

uneasy at nite
sleep
upon

a mountain
full
of

giant trees in
macmillan
park

the touristos
feed my
cat

pack their
bags
nd

drive like
hell
to

the next stop
in hope
b.c.

after crossing
the channel
sea

nd the hitch
hikenest
blues

you ever heard
coming on
down

nd everyone's
laffin out
the

rain upon
black
wet

pavement drivin
hard nd
fast

gettin off'n
trying to
make it

nd not really gettin
anywhere fast
like

big steve

rubs his hands
together
for

the forty fifth
time enough
for

one more deal
before the
store

closes man i'm in
for this round
of carpet

sweeping nd all the
city cleaners
going out

of business after
this has been
run thru

the bay street
slop pail
one

more time more time more time

xxiv

you told me late one nite
you were good at
your job

of course your line
of work was
helping

i was afraid to tell
you mine was in
despair

silver nd black

it took three nites
to get this
down

her bracelets are made of
silver nd black
silver nd black
silver nd black
silver nd black

i don't have any excuses
good lines are slow work

thunder bay

out
in the
bay where

the
giant
sleeps

the
waves
are silent

here
along
the shore

where
the old
people are

buried
they lick
the rocks nd

the wind
continues into
the third season

while
the chamber
of commerce asks

six bits
for a lectured
tour of the bones

still the
great mystery
is not explained

silver
sparkles all
along the coast

tofino b.c.

land of
mountains

hovering
dead volcanoes

nd rain
by the sea

nd salmon
fishing at the
mouth of the river
of the great
ocean nd north
wind on the shore

beating
hell outta the
Indian fishermen

in the
off season
winter months

here
where the
raven meets

the coast
nd the bird
of flying thunder

dies nd
the great circle
once again completed

in the
spirit of
the people

i cannot say
when I passed here last
for it was long ago

nd now my
north country
is calling me back

xvi

As the tiny stream
melts before the shining sun,
her thoughts turn to spring.

xvii

She sees the firefly
along the shore at night and
o how her love shines.

xviii

As the autumn moon
sinks by her open window,
she knows he is near.

xvix

She gathers snowflakes
beside the frozen river,
candles in her hand.

joseph

(hinmaton yalatkit)

sound
of the
high water

dips
down thru
the mountain

rushes
to me while
the sun sleeps

storm
clouds meet
getting it all

together
in the late
nite wind dance

but i
swear all i
could hear was thunder

thunder
rolling in
the mountains

23

earth nites

i've been away so long
away from this land
nd home

i called a single
silver band of
circles

where the moon
climbs on to
the brite

side of the sun she
wore a mask nd
saw

the ancient ones
spinnin away the
lites

i see her there jupiter
can i ever see
her

again she said there's
no need to hurry
now

i see the raven man
i won't
need

to get the story told
around fires late
at nite

nd want the blazing
trail between
the stars

earth i've been away
from her too
long

the planet jupiter star
is closer
than

you think it's
all beyond
you

i can see that i
can see that
i can

see there's no more rest now

taking down the big blue

take her down
where the
silver

bells are ringing
big blue nd
all the

flowing nites
in shining
steel

peel off 50's like
the wind takes
down maple

leaves in the fall
guy who manages
to get it

all together
before he
gets

strung out to dry
by the CIBC
taking

back a second on
the old nd
broke

down homestead
man i can't
seem to

get off anymore
in screwing
people

left right nd
centre star
for the

way things might have been
if we'd all kept
our shit

together instead of
draining the
old pot

dry dry dry dry dry dry dry dry

hangin on

i'm hangin on
to yer
old

sparklin star nd
astral moon
again

orange flame
kissin the
ice

betrayed just as judas
felt the
auric

fingers wrapped
around his
throat

tryina make it out
to where yer
blue

eyes struck the snow
nd all the blood
flyin

everywhere nd old man
winter hittin
again

nd again and again
like some
crack

addict nd me
reelin nd
rollin

like the last
dance was
some

kind of a crazy shuffle
down the street
nd all of

all of a sudden who
appears but
lookin

down at good old paris
my favourite
city

clothes fallin off
in front of the
tower

nd her wrappin
her arms
around

wrapped them all around
my naked
flight

her blonde hair
blowin in my
eyes

nd blowin in
my eyes
nd

tangled
up all tang
led in my face

did you know anything at all

did
you know
her hair
was blonde

or did
you even
care it
was long

and did
you ever
speak of
her beauty

i don't
suppose
you knew
she died

strangled
in her
long
blonde
beauty

when she
found out
no one
was watching

so long now

it has been
so long
now

and when i
think of
you

the days when
all i
knew

was blonde on
the sun
blonde

lites in my
brain and
eye

exploding
in my
face

blood dripping
from the
deep

dark image
and dust
but

well it has
been so
long

now

xiii

eyes
      solemn
      black
      unyielding

only
      possible
      entry
      thru

a diagonal
      slit
      in the
      left iris

mutilation
      b'cos
      people
      will say

she really wasn't looking back

shaman and the raven

that sideways glance
you happen to
notice

over yer shoulder
when yer not
really

noticin her lowered eye
level stare that's
not direct

except when you try to look
her in the left
eye

payin attention to
what it is
she's

sayin to everyone
reachin out
to

get the spirit nd the feel
of the east wind
blowin

comin in under
the door nd
alley

while the whole auditorium
gets that
feelin

feelin that she's gonna
do it again nd
the lites

sorta start poppin for
everyone to see
if

they're gonna be recognized
almost right
away

nd then you start gettin
scared nd kinda
stretch

eyed lookin around
even she's
been

shocked by the outrage
of such old
tricks

nd all of a sudden he's
there too the
black

raven himself walkin
nd talkin kinda
almost

too low for anyone
to hear what
he's

sayin nd now she's prayin
nd sayin her verses
to the bear

nd protection altho it's not
really needed anymore
cos it's

too late to start over he's
holding on to her arm
nd feelin

the power of long ago nd
old time ways
now

she knows she's not the only
one seein the blue
flashes

as it's all explained but
not explained
enough

to make you wonder what
the score is then
the

shaman searches the room
again nd again
with

her brown eyes
twitchin nd
burnin

nd searchin for that
whispy feelin
hiding

between conversations nd coughs
knowin it's the
trickster

watchin words nd breath
get mixed up nd
delivered

kind of gently into every
unsuspecting ear
nd mouth

Prayer of the Mystic Warrior

Oh great mystery
And man above,
Hear me now
For I stand before you
Humble and obedient.
Make me strong
To fight my enemies.
Give me strength
To protect my loved ones.
Help me
Overcome my weaknesses.

    Make

      Me

        Worthy

xxii

tell me again what
the oppressed
look like

i'm sure i can dig up enough
anguish nd despair
to go

around

xxvi

she took one last look in
my direction
shook

her head nd returned
to studyin her
map

while i practiced the
two step of
despair

dancin nd dancin way into the nite

copacabana tourists

on the promenade walk
of copacabana i
told

my boy what the colours
were created
for

nd how they represented
three peoples of
brasil

the red nd black nd white

the red of course was for
us the real
people

the black was for
the black
people

nd the white was for
the portuguese
peoples

all who came to live in
this land long
ago

i could tell he was
curious
nd

lookin down studyin the walk
like some kind of
an ant

with a magnifying
glass in his
hand

askin me again if we could
go to the beach
now

howlin at the moon

take the moon
nd take a star
when you don't
know who you are

paint the picture in your hand
nd roll on home

take my fear
nd take the hunger
take my body
when i'm younger

paint the picture in your hand
nd roll on home

take my ghost
nd make the claim
stake it out
to feel the pain

paint the picture in your hand
nd roll on home

take the moon
nd make it talk
take your soul out
make it walk

paint the picture in your hand
nd roll on home

take my anguish
take the air
make it into
my despair

paint the picture in your hand
nd roll on home

take my anger
nd the greed
make it into
what you need

paint the picture in your hand
nd roll on home

take my pride
nd all my joy
take my woman
nd my boy

paint the picture in your hand
nd roll on home

paint the picture once again
i'm rollin home

for linda

i saw exertion
on your
face

nd lines from
long
ago

i thought i saw a candle
burning from
your lips

nd smoke that
was like
snow

i heard
a whispered
tired breath

it sounded
just like
dew

if i could find
a tear nd
star

i'd wash them
all away
for you

i'd wash them all away for you

spirit spinnin

my spirit spins in two
concentric
circles

one going forward
the other in reverse

doing a delicate dance
down the street
in the nite

spinnin nd weavin its
own peculiar type of patterns

till i meet yer
long blonde
beauty

unfolding in the dark nd the
circles kinda start shakin nd

slidin outta kilter
like a worm
in

a storm that's
floppin all over

nd i'm gettin up
off the
sidewalk

nose bludgeoned nd bleedin again

eagle's work

eagle strikes her prey
out of the air
with

one screaming blow
of blood nd
talon

swift nd clean nd proud

i torture this page
for hours
til

finally my soul stumbles
out sick of being the
official witness

starts walkin nd talkin nd dancin right out loud

south wheel

is all those majik
fires lit late
in the
nite

is lions nd
foxes nd
bear

is orange nd red
amber nd
white

is washin your eyes with
the sun nd the
lite

is sweetgrass
nd cinnamon
cedar nd
gold

is dancin with love with
love til your
old

for donald marshall

i've no secret old
time answer in
my hand

i've no majik justice in my sand

to challenge all
the inmate
time

to pray beside the sacred pine

i've no blazin fire trail
to sear the
wounds

nd close the ruptured aura burns

but seek her now nd
make it
end

seek her now nd see my friend

o great bear of the southern wheel
o great bear of the southern wheel
o great bear of the southern wheel
o great bear of the southern wheel

take the power
nd the
earth

take this breath to heal the hurt

take the power
nd your
healing

take the breath nd take this feeling

travel now in
breath nd
wind

travel now nd take the wind

travel now in
earth nd
land

travel now nd take the land

clothe him in
a yellow
gold

touch the pain nd make it old

checkin out the bondage scroll

i didn't want the job
nd said it wasn't
my area

of expertise as if i
had an area of
expertise

but the women agreed nd said i would be the one

so they started explainin it
bout the men makin
them ill

nd tryina solve their
problems with
gravel nd

shovels used during the egyptian days

least that's how I've been
advised to write
it down

i'm talking about when
the pyramids were
built

the slavery nd sweat
piled on the
rocks

nd no one listenin to the pain anymore

nd bein the official
scribe of this
tale

i'm only supposed to
be checkin the
list

of everyone on the chain gang

but i can't help noticin
there's not a women's
name anywhere on
the overseer's
scroll

please be advised

i love you madly
i can't help myself
i have always loved you
i watched you naked every nite
i have no honour
i would have talked you into bed
every time i met you if i had the chance
i am passion's lieutenant for you
i am the sorcerer of lust
don't ever ask me into your house late at nite
i would dissolve off all your clothes
with my majik
while your children nd husband were sleeping
i would give up my black mountain bike
to lie between your thighs for one nite
i would enshrine your body
with a thousand candles nd caresses
i would drink your beauty until i passed out
i am more psychotic than your craziest client
i can never be cured
i will be like this forever
so i hope this is perfectly clear to you
locking your door at nite won't help
i can astral travel nd doors mean
nothing to me
you can never escape from me
i will be the closet ghost at your death bed
the only way you can save yourself
is to become a shaman like me
only then will you learn to love me
only then can you know all about me
only then can you possibly get free of me
you might even have more power than me
but i doubt it

for i am raven
trickster nd magician
i don't practice high majik
i am high majik
no one talks to you like this
i am the only one who talks to you like this
no one is entranced with you like this
you know who wrote this
you know who i am
i know you are smiling
nd you'll never be the same again

i won't be able

i won't be able to die now
only honourable men
are allowed that glory

i told everyone your secret
    unashamed

like some shabby pervert
on the six o'clock
edition of the news

i exposed myself to the nation
    nd bowed

unaware your beauty lay
there broken
nd still

unable to recognize any of the applause

a raven's trick

there's a river that's
flowin with
colours

in a dream where the bear went to hide

there's a ribbon of
sweetgrass around
you

in a dream where the elk never cried

there's a blue raven
feather beside
you

there's a turquoise of
stone in your
hand

there's a shadow of
love in your
doorway

in a dream made of silver nd sand

there's a moonstone
trapped in your
beauty

there's a pocket of
newly found
gold

there's a man in the
nite who was
waiting

in your dream that
could never
get old

in your dream that could never get old

down on the yucatan

down on the yucatan
that's where
i

met some 40,000 years
of confidence
i

thought was only a
hallucination
i

could see it in his
nite brown
i

could see it on the face
of that old mayan
i

could tell you he knew sean
was my only child
i

almost laffed at when
he told me
i

was seven kids
behind him
i

could feel his mournful
feeling in my
i

was really something
special when
i

saw the jungle lion
nd i saw that she
was flyin nd
i

saw the eagle
cryin nd
i

saw her way up flyin
in the sky
i

could see her i could
feel her
i

could see that he was
seein nd
i

had his hand in mine
he wasn't dyin
i

went down to the
old yucatan
i

couldn't catch her
beauty in my
i

just took her power
in me
i

took her power in me
nd i fly
i

don't know why he spoke
no english
i

don't know why he spoke
no spanish
i

just guess he wouldn't speak
outside his mother
tongue
i

told him i refused to speak
any of that old mayan
i

saw down on the yucatan
nd that's where
i

said i just come
down here
i

just come down to yucatan
nd watch the deer nd pheasant
i

just come on down alone here
i just come on down
alone here nd
i fly

smoke nd thyme

they told me
to stop wearin
that old medicine shirt
to the office

nd i agreed this time

but i never told them
about the medicine bag
i made late in the nite

about the cedar flame
the smoke
nd the thyme

i'm not in charge of this ritual

i'm not in charge of this
sun dance anymore
i'm hangin here
completely out of it
the lawyers nd therapists
have taken over
my breasts are pierced
nd writhin in the blood
nd pain
i'm not that brave you know
that's why my children
nd woman were
taken from me
that's why i'm takin it on alone again
i never did any of those purification rituals
that's probably why this isn't working
nd hallucinations start sneakin
into my work, i can't say home
because i don't have a home
i live in a room
making medicine bags nd
wonderin if the silver strands
nd gems i'm puttin in them will do the trick
i escape temporarily at nite catching
my breath at donut & pizza shops
where nobody talks nd everyone just eats
munchin nd chewin nd swallowin down
hunger in the nite
hah! despair wouldn't have the nerve to come
waltzin through the door here
it would be devoured whole
in one fat gulp
they're all lookin at me wonderin why

i'm so skinny nd still losing weight
they know i'm not one of them
but i'm there every nite
shakin over another cup of coffee
tired nd numb from another day of torture
i'm glad when the sun goes down
nd the crazy cool of dark comes
b'cos there's hardly anywhere left to hide
nd they'll find me in the mornin
nd drag me back to the dance
in front of the sun
i wish i knew how long this was gonna take
but there's always tonite
nd ah! there's always linda
always linda waitin in the nite
with smoky topaz eyes
with smokin lips nd thighs
pressed like a gem
from the earth
into mine
but even she's started lockin
her door at nite

if i ever heard

if i ever heard
your love had gone pale

i would come out of this wilderness
with ojibiway majik
    for you

if i ever heard
your love had gone without rain

i would come out of this wilderness
with my ojibiway river
    for you

if i ever heard
your love had gone in the sea

i would come of this wilderness
with ojibiway earth
    for you

if i ever heard
your love had gone in the nite

i would come out of this wilderness
with my ojibiway stars
    for you

just one nite

i didn't understand
why your husband
got so upset

after all both you nd i
know there was only
that one time

only that one nite

there was never any trip around the world
we didn't abandon our children
or run off to paris
or hide out in mexico
or sneak off to brasil
or camp out on the pacific rim
we didn't crucify anyone in the process
least i didn't
nd i never gave up
on any of my friends
we never killed ourselves
or cashed in any of our savings bonds
or jumped out of the office window
some sunny afternoon
after lunch

nd i think he's completely
full of shit
i never would have left that poem
written by a brit
for you
everybody knows what i might have left there
nd you know it too
yeats for tradition
cohen for a bit of good old victimized humour
something by twain for an outright belly laff
nd yes i mighta even a tried
my own sloppy hand

for a bit of cosmic emotion
plastered on that page

willow woman

i didn't want to get involved
like this
with this willow woman
prehistoric dancer
from some paleolithic age
all i wanted was to have
my aching eyes washed down
with the birch nd the rain
or some majikal cleanser
right off the shelf
would have been enough
i swear that's all I wanted
i'm not hard to get along with
but now i'm stuck with this
nd now i'm haunted with this
nitemare walkin around
beside me in broad daylight
sun shinin everywhere
nd me actin like there's nothin
strange happenin here
but the dogs
the dogs are givin us away
growlin nd snappin like that
every time we walk by

yucatan jaguar

but how
will i meet
the jaguar in the nite
i asked the toltec woman
lookin at me in despair
with these old weapons
that don't work anymore
i mean these broken arrowheads
nd cracked lance
lyin in the sun
bleached white
as the bones
that haunt them

there didn't seem to be
much of a choice
runnin through
the terror
nd jungle vines
hangin all over you
like a doe on fire
tryina catch her panic
til you finally
shout out your death song
shakin your head free
of every bad dream
that ever crept into your bed
nd you start to sweat
that steamy jungle sweat
boilin in the dark
nd the great fracture takes place
comin apart
nd moon whimperin in the corner
like somebody's kicked dog
smoke nd fire everywhere

chokin the hell outta this trance
you're in while you're hangin on to the edge
flirtin insidiously with
more horror nd power
than any mayan priest
could ever have imagined
nd finally you know how to meet her
finally you know how to see her
nd finally you know
you know how to stay alive
nd you call it all in
the raven nd fire
sorcery nd majik
nd meet her beauty
collidin nd crashin with her
tearin nd growlin nd coffin
out the only lung of breath
you had left
feelin the claw in your gut
as she works those hind legs
nd fang deep in your shoulder
writhin nd screamin
til you see it
in the clear of it all
nd the white of the sky
you see the blue raven feather
the blue raven feather
floatin nd glidin
floatin nd glidin
down to the green
down to the
green
coral bay
where you first met
the jaguar

aztecs nd sun

a quarter to ten
and four ravens
flap recklessly through
the alley way
squawkin nd sweatin like
they're talkin about
some kind of crazy
old time sign

of the flight veers
off to the left
hot nd high over my head

i'm superstitious as hell
makin sure there's four
of them
watchin the whole place
creepin nd crawlin with those
god damn
caterpillars

all over the
handrails along
the sidewalk
nd that old summer
smell
oozin outta the walkway
fryin in the air
just like
chapultapec park
early in the mornin
before the heat
of the crowd moves in
nd starts firin up
the concrete
i'm standin on
like another boilin
aztec temple
nd sun

movin back to mexico

i could move back to mexico
you know
linda

nd learn to sing
nd play a guitar
maybe
drink tequila
or hang out as a local

nobody would know the difference
i mean brown skin nd all

maybe etch out your image
in one of those small
silver shops
around
taxco

but it probably wouldn't work out

i mean you lookin over yer shoulder
every time you went out
at nite wonderin
if i was
back

crazy nd runnin after you
in the middle of all
those years
waitin

nd dreamin those old time raven
dreams of fire nd
time

cracked open like glass
on a stone
nd

i know yer not really in to
turquoise nd silver
nd my hands are
gettin kinda
shaky now
anyway

to be carvin out yer beauty
with silver
nd sand

game trail run

i can't trust
my eyes anymore
or that warm feelin
on my face

it's hard to imagine
that old yucatan sun findin
its way up here from so far south

getting caught up
in pourin out all that blue
in the sky nd river floodin her breath

nd hand with quicksilver
flowin nd her workin nd blowin nd
workin the silver with whispers nd sand

comin down like salt grains
stashed away on some old game trail
yer poundin down on the dead run comin to rest

on one knee nd her tryina
stop the bleedin while yer whole body's
exposed to nothin but the heat nd dust finally

hittin the snare in full
flight like that nd crashin to the
ground as you break the noose in the fall nd

coolin down nd
coolin down nd her coolin
down the heat nd coolin it all down

til it's
hard to imagine
that old yucatan sun

hard to imagine
the quicksilver workin
like that nd her blowin the
silver nd that old yucatan sun findin

its way up here from so far south

earth fractures

mornin
time again to
breathe nd tryina
figure out

what's happenin
to the air nd summer dust
foldin into the sun rise

i can't get her
outta my mind
that park way down in mexico city
chapultapec park
chapultapec park
chapultapec park
chapultapec park

it's gettin to be like some kind of a chant
like a chant lightly callin
what really floored me
later that afternoon

sittin down to have a coffee
at my own table
starin at the cupboard door
nd again the fracture
happenin and sittin
there still as stone
was the grasshopper
clingin to the door
inverted position

this can't be so
but catchin her in my hand
nd throwin her out the door
i knew that it was
i'm glad i know about these things
goin on when no one bothers
to take a look
nd find out that
maybe someone else would think
they're dreamin here

nd i know what this is
this ain't no dream
i know what carlos meant
i mean him
foolin around with those old
yaqui ways like he couldn't quite
get it all together
right away
but finally gettin up to speed
walkin through the fractures
seein the grasshopper
in more ways than
one

every magician knows

every magician knows
what to do
i mean

practising
with those images
in the mirror
every nite
nd

catching that
cloudy change
from raven to man
from raven to man
from man to raven
from raven to mist

listenin to margaret
nd walkin clear through
that gaelic breath

talkin about some
old pagan holyday
in december
over in Ireland

til you've walked
just about
every county on the south
side of the island

keepin it all
together for just
one more time
nd her wantin
the turquoise
nd wantin
the silver
nd tryina find it in
all that green

i said
nd you know
it can only happen
down there
i mean down there
on the boulevard
down there
right in chapultapec park
next to the grasshopper
next to the toltecs
nd next to the jaguar
walkin around
in the sun

every time it happens

every time it
happens
now

i manage to call
out the
jaguar

spittin nd coffin
growlin nd
clawin

after the beauty
there in
every

eye that ever watched
over me in
the nite

shakin their heads
in disbelief
wonderin

how a raven manages
to stay alive
in

the midst of
all that
terror

nd fang devourin the lite

lite nd silver

for mairead

lovely colleen you
are pining
late

in the nite for your
gaelic father
nd love

by your side
long ago
when

all you knew was folded
in an emerald nd
a gem

how could i ever give it back to
you know i'd take on almost
any kind of work

take this green
from my wilderness
take it from my achin tongue

take this fire
from my camp on the trail
take it from my winter snow nd hail

take this field
from every hill nd run
take it from my forest mist nd sun

take this heart
from all my land take it
from the moonlight silver in your hand

the moonlight
silver found in sand
the kind a tear nd beauty understand

showin up as a raven has its drawbacks

not knowing what
to expect
i

showed up as a raven as
usual all in
black

lookin really slick
nd that fine
coal dust

floatin around in the air
everywhere she
stood

there actually not
recognizing
the

disguise even tho
i said that's
what

i am that's what I am that's
what i am a raven
nd i said

that's what i am
but not that
many

really believe in magicians anymore
nd gettin all nervous
like that

then the fracture openin up
nd that old majik
trick jumpin

directly into the daylight
nd the prayin startin
nd power

crossin over the street takin
beauty by the hand nd
her lookin

at the yucatan just outside
the window starin
in nd

askin all about that steamy jungle
changin from the desert
into green

gettin an eye full nd tryina do
all that talkin with
a trickster's mouth
knowin full well that
showin up as a raven has its drawbacks

toltec runner nd gold

first there was
that climb
in the sun
scorchin nd sweatin
prayin nd poundin
up the way
i thought
would never
come to any kind of a halt
the trip i mean
gettin over that
old moctezuma trail
was some kind of a trick

like that runner comin in
from the coast
up the road sinkin
in silver nd stone ·
blue green feather
nd headdress floatin
nd glidin caressin the air
nd feelin it
all in the blisterin wind
on your back
movin only like the runner can
workin your way up that ridge
nd mountain range
never really lookin behind
but catchin the white
of the coast
periodically comin around
another bend nd twist
weavin nd workin out all
the exertion in your breath

breakin out nd finally
breakin out
onto the high plain
all that way from the coast
bringin in those fresh crustaceans
for the last feast nd all
the next day
knowin you're almost there
from the coast
outside vera cruz
to the great city
the boilin city

mexihco
mexihco
mexihco

one single overnite
run hardly anyone ever even heard about
or even cared to remember
only to find
only to find
what she really wanted
blazin in the heat nd run
what she really wanted
was all that blazin nd burnin
blazin nd burnin
toltec runner nd gold

dreamcatcher nd dancer

when i
danced with
the people
beneath the black
nd dream
in her eye
nd the raven
dancer

i couldn't believe anymore
i saw her smile
i couldn't
i just couldn't
couldn't
believe
i saw her smile
nd the fox dancer
in front of me
drum poundin
in my head
so i couldn't
think anymore
in this kind
of a trance

i could only feel
anymore
could only feel it
the dreamcatcher
the silver
nd the stars
all full in my hand

for bertholde carter

there's a garden
of blue found
beside
you

in a
breath by the
lead nd the moth

there's a new field
of silver
beside
you

by your
glove with the
rose nd the moss

there's a forest
of green all
beside
you

with your
love where the
deer went to cross

with your love where the deer went to cross

toltec boy

there's no
majik
in

turquoise nd
silver
like

you've been told

there's no
power
in

the pale
white
moon

the one my people hold

there's only
sean nd
me

my toltec
boy
nd

jaguars made of gold

from yucatan
from yucatan

that jaguar
down from
yucatan

the ones made all of gold

day break run

comin
back into
that day break

run nd mist
standin still nd
smokin all along the low

spots not yet
lite but lite enough
to see your way through this

earth mother's
shroud nd veil comin
up everywhere you look the moon

kinda pale nd
white hangin out
in front full nd round

pumpin along at 120
nd nobody's lookin at much
this time of the mornin except me

checkin the mirror
behind nd tryina put a
hundred miles or a bit more

of green
belt between you
nd the cloud nd carter

standin
there beneath
the bustin toltec sun

all red
nd crawlin up
behind the trees

takin that
raven on the windshield
 like that nd prayin to the iron

to the copper nd glass
to hold this all together
for at least another forty minutes

of my time
nd warm feelin
on my back pullin away

to the west
nd pullin away
til she bursts out

all that
gold breathin out
all that gold nd changin

changin every line
that ever danced at daybreak
into another golden ojibiway sun

from the marino waltz

love is pleasin
  love is pleasin
    love is pleasin
      love is pleasin
    love is pleasin
  love is pleasin
love is pleasin
  love is pleasin
    love is pleasin
      love is pleasin
        love is pleasin
          love is pleasin
            love is pleasin
              love is pleasin
                love is pleasin
                  love is pleasin
                    love is pleasin
                      love is pleasin
                    love is pleasin
                  love is pleasin
                love is pleasin
              love is pleasin
            love is pleasin
          love is pleasin
        love is pleasin
      love is pleasin
    love is pleasin
      love is pleasin
        love is pleasin
          love is pleasin
            love is pleasin
              love is pleasin
                love is pleasin
                o yes it is

dreamcatcher rings

pieces fallin
outta the
air

now like findin
a way to
float

along nd sorta goin
like a viennese
waltz

not really outta
synch with
raven

wings nd dreamcatcher rings
although i don't remember
the sayin
exactly

i once heard
you say
i

love you
love you
love you
love you

like i never waltzed before

i
love
you

were yuh true

were yuh true
were yuh true
were yuh true
were yuh true
were yuh true
were yuh true
were yuh true
were yuh true

when yuh hung
before the toltec
sun nd gold
were yuh true
to every breath
yuh gulped

the nite
yuh cornered
the jaguar
down

nd did yuh thank
the air
for lettin yuh live

nd did you thank
the power
for lettin yuh give

it all up
nd did yuh
come clear
through that fracture

like any other shaman
would with only
majik nd silver
majik nd silver
majik nd silver
majik nd silver

naked on your breast

Spirit Warrior Raven

A long time ago, in the land of the Anishnawbe, there was a man whose name was Raven. I met him on a winter trail a long way from here. He looked very tired and was suffering from many wounds. His clothes were torn and dirty and blood stained. I helped him to my campfire to rest a while.

We sat by the fire for a long time. Neither of us talked. The Raven man fell asleep. I melted some snow and began to wash the dirt and blood away from his wounds. The Raven man slept for two suns. During this time I kept a small fire burning and repaired his clothes and brushed them down with cedar boughs.

On the night of the second day, the Raven man awoke. He was somewhat cleaner and some of his wounds had been dressed. He looked across the fire, and reached out with his hand. His face was grey as ash. He took my arm and held it for a moment. I was surprised by the strength of his grasp. He whispered, barely audible to me, "Thank you, my friend." I reached for the water I had melted from the snow and handed it to him. He took a long drink, raising his eyes to the stars, as if he was searching for the distance and direction he had yet to go. When he handed me the empty cup, he nodded his thanks and sat up to warm himself over the fire.

The Raven man began to speak, but did not look up as he started to warm his hands over the fire. "Many moons ago, I was sent to the desert where life and death meet. I had no desire to go there, but had been horribly betrayed and left there to die, or so I thought. Do you know of this place?", he asked me, looking directly into my eyes. I answered that I had not been there, but had heard of such a place.

"I wandered in the desert for a long time, without water or food. The sun was scorching and merciless and finally beat me to the ground. I thought I was going to die. But, at that moment I was suddenly on a ridge that overlooked the entrance to two valleys. I was refreshed, but very confused, and stood there overlooking the entrance way. Then, the great mystery spoke to me and asked me why I had come to this place. The voice was very gentle and seemed to be all around me. I said that I didn't want to be there but had been betrayed and left in the desert to die. The great mystery was silent for a while but finally spoke again. 'This desert is the cross-road between life and death. No one can stay in the desert. I see that they are brought to the entrance of these two valleys. Do you wish to enter the valley of death, Raven man?'

"I answered 'No...' with uncertainty.

"Again the great mystery was silent for some time. He finally spoke and told me that it was good that I chose life and reminded me of something I couldn't seem to remember any more, from a time when I lived in the valley of life. 'I heard you one day. It was a warm sunny day on the high plains. You were with your brother and made a sun vow to take his child as your own and to protect that child's life with your life. I was afraid you had forgotten.'

"I fell to my knees with my head in my hands and wept. I was so ashamed I wept for a long time at the cross-roads. The great mystery seemed to disappear. Finally a warm south wind came up, cooling and soothing my face. I could feel her smile and soon was able to stand up again.

"The great mystery returned and spoke to me again. He explained that I could return to the valley of life again but I would have to cross a battle plain. There were many fierce warriors there and that I should pray and prepare myself. There was a possibility that I would not be able to cross this plain and that, since no one could stay in the desert, I would be forced to go into the valley of death. Here there were no barriers, and one simply had to walk down the easy path into the valley. On the battle plain, many people were pinned down and the warriors from this plain attacked them every day. They had been there a long time. No one knew how long the fighting would go on.

"I started down toward the plain the next day. It was a hideous place. The clouds were black and dark and the feeling of evil was everywhere. I began to feel worse and worse.

The great mystery had told me that warriors on this plain would always come from the east, from the direction of the valley of life. I marched for three days across the plain. It appeared to get longer and longer as I marched across it, yet I remembered that from the ridge, it only seemed a short distance to the valley of life. On the fourth day, I saw dust on the horizon. I knew the warriors of the plain were here.

"I took the lengthy leather thong from my medicine bag and the bone stake. I picked out the most even piece of ground I could see and staked myself out, ankle to the thong. I could not return to the valley of death and the great mystery had warned of retreat on this plain. Retreat on the plain of battle means the plain will never end. This is not an ordinary plain that you can walk across. When your carry your weapons on to this plain, it grows very long and you may travel a long time before you meet its warriors. When you begin to retreat, you will become lost as the plain grows larger. It is best to meet the warriors and stand your ground here.

"The warriors were mounted and rode up close, to within shouting distance. They were fierce looking and proud as the great mystery had said they would be. Many of them looked to be great warriors. I counted the eagle feathers. There were three, four and five. My heart began to sink. The warriors kept arriving. There were surely a hundred. I thought that I would die here.

"When it seemed that they had all arrived, they started to jeer and shout. 'The battle will be good,' they shouted. 'At last, a dog soldier,' they screamed as they brandished their weapons. One of the warriors moved ahead of the others. He was very old and ugly, and talked as if some foul bile ran through his veins. 'We have a worthy warrior to meet you, Raven man.' The old man motioned with his lance. A great black horse leapt forward, snorting and rearing. The warrior who rode him had painted his face completely black. He wore four black eagle feathers. His lance looked like gold.

"'This is the mighty warrior Betrayal!' the old man shouted with a terrible cry.

"As the warrior charged I steadied my lance. My blow was intended for the chest, but it seemed to go right through the warrior as if he was air. Then my own shoulder was torn with his lance. It burned with pain and I screamed in agony as I fell to the ground. I couldn't get up for a long time. The other warriors let out a great whoop as the warrior Betrayal rode back to the group. My head was reeling with the pain. The old man motioned with his lance again. Another warrior jumped forward, as terrible as the first.

101

"'This is Rejection!' laughed the old man.

The warrior's lance pierced my leg. I swung my war club in rage. It was like chopping the air again. The pain screamed through my head.

"Again and again the warriors charged. I couldn't understand why I wasn't dead yet. I couldn't seem to strike them, yet every time they struck it seemed like a fresh blow. I stayed there day after day. Their names were Revenge, Anger, Hate, Despair, and Depression...

"One day as I stood up, I picked up my bow and closed my eyes. 'Raven!' I cried out with my inner voice. 'Give me your sharp eyes today. Let my arrow find its mark. Let me begin to end this battle,' I begged.

"A single warrior came forward and prepared for his charge. I went to one knee to steady my aim and cried 'Raven, help me now!' I let the arrow fly. Everything seemed to be happening very slowly. I could see the arrow soar straight and true and find its mark in the warrior's chest. I heard an awful scream as I stood up. I couldn't contain my horror as the face of the warrior changed to the face of the loved one who had betrayed me. My stomach turned and I threw up as the warrior rode by. I turned and watched the warrior ride past until he faded away to nothing. There was deathly silence as I stared into the deserted plain.

"Suddenly a great shout rose from the group of warriors. I turned to see them all mounting and preparing to charge. I knew I was going to die and threw down my weapons to face them. The first warrior charged and counted coup with his hand, striking my shoulder. The second struck the side of my head with his hand and rode past. More and more warriors counted coup until they just began to ride past without touching me any more. I turned to watch them ride away until they faded into the dust.

"When I looked again to the east, I saw the valley of life. It seemed to be very close and I started for it right away. As I entered the valley it became winter and I saw that I was a long way from my home. That is how I came to meet you on this trail.

"My heart is sick from this battle and these wounds pain me very much. I am weary and I thank you for the fire and your kindness."

Then, the Raven man left my fire.